£10

A Wished-For Song

A Portrait of
Jeff Buckley

Photographs and Interviews
by Merri Cyr

 inc.

"A Wished-for Song" by Jelaluddin Rumi, translated by Coleman Barks,
with John Moyne, from *The Essential Rumi* (New York: HarperCollins,
1994, 1997).

Photo of Jeff Buckley and Andrea Lisle in photo collage on opposing page
by Lely Constantinople

Published by Hal Leonard Corporation
7777 W. Bluemound Rd.
P.O. Box 13819
Milwaukee, WI 53213

New York City Editorial Offices:
Hal Leonard Corporation
151 West 46th Street, 8th Floor
New York, NY 10036

Printed in U.S.A.

First Edition

Designed by Merri Cyr
Visit Merri Cyr online at **www.merricyr.com**

Library of Congress Cataloging-in-Publication Data
Cyr, Merri, 1964-
   A wished-for song : a portrait of Jeff Buckley / photographs and
interviews by Merry Cyr.--1st ed.
      p. cm.
   ISBN 0-634-03595-9
      1. Buckley, Jeff, 1966-1997--Portraits. 1. Title.

ML88.B78 C97 2002
782.42166'092--dc21
[B]

10 9 8 7 6 5 4 3 2

2002068459

Australian Music Trade
Hal Leonard Australia Pty Ltd
22 Taunton Drive
Cheltenham East, VIC 3192
Ph: 61 (0)3 9585 3300
Fax: 61 (0)3 9585 3399
E-mail: aussales@halleonard.com

Australian Book Trade
Gary Allen Pty Ltd
9 Cooper Street
Smithfield, NSW 2164
Ph: 61 (0)2 9725 2933
Fax: 61 (0)2 9609 6155
http://www.garyallen.com.au

Exclusive sale and distribution in North America and
the rest of the world excluding Europe and Australia.
Visit Hal Leonard online at **http://www.halleonard.com**

Exclusive sales and distribution in the UK and EU:
Omnibus Press 8/9 Frith Street London W1D 3JB
http://www.omnibuspress.com

(JEFF BUCKLEY)

ROMAIN
DREAMS LIVE IN THE THROAT
2/13/95 Jeff Buckley
LARRY MULLENS
4-EVER!

Demon Internet
30 day free trial call
0800 027 0127

OCTOBER?   Sept. 17/98

Please send anything on
Jeff Buckley you can.
Anything would be great to
have and remember him by

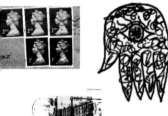

JEFF BUCKLEY

ELLEN'S SOUL FOOD
"good eatin'"

Interview participants:

Steve Berkowitz	A&R, Columbia Records
Dave Lory	manager
Sam Way	international publicity, artist relations, Columbia Records
Penny Arcade	friend
Jack Bookbinder	management team
Howard Wuelfing	publicity advisor, Columbia Records
George Stein	lawyer
Leah Reid	friend
Brenda Kahn	friend
Inger Lorre	friend
Joan Wasser	friend
Andria Lisle	friend
Ellen Cavolina	friend
Michael Tighe	guitarist, Jeff Buckley Band
Matt Johnson	drummer, Jeff Buckley Band
Nick Hill	WFMU Radio DJ

"I'll be your muse."

— *Jeff Buckley*

The first time I met Jeff Buckley I was on a photo assignment for a New York–based publication called *Paper* magazine. It was for a small article and I hadn't heard of the musician, but the editor there, David, thought I might be interested in the job. I accepted. On the day of the shoot, I went to Jeff's apartment, and with the help of my friend Eric (assistant for the day), we dragged my gear up to his fourth-floor walk-up. While I set up the lights and figured out some angles the guys started talking musical shop, and Eric made himself comfortable browsing through Jeff's CD and tape collection. I coerced Jeff into the other room and we took some shots in his top hat and trademark flannel shirt, then to the hallway and roof for a finale NY skyline shot. Even from that first shoot I felt a definite sense of play and a willingness on the part of Jeff to be open to experimentation that made photographing him an adventure. Of course, he was always checking you out, giving you that Scorpio scan thang, but when we were doing the actual creative work he was amazingly accessible and present. Connected.

After photographing Jeff I definitely knew that he was a good artist, even though I hadn't seen him play. I brought a couple of prints from the shoot and we went to see him perform at Sin-é. Wow. All the girls (and a few guys too) were blubbering, particularly during his rendition of "Hallelujah." One guy and a guitar. He could seduce a crowd in any direction and they would follow.

After the show, he was hanging out outside and I handed him the box of photos. He looked at me like he didn't recognize me and gave me the scan. "Don't you remember me? I took your photo last week. I made you a couple." He opened the box and his face lit up. Stoneman to goofboy in a second flat. Big hug.

Some months later I arrived home one day to find a mountain of messages blinking frantically on my answering machine. I started listening to them, and it was like one long run-on sentence interrupted by an occasional gasping beep from the machine. Jeff was going to record his first EP, *Live at Sin-é*, and he wanted me to photograph it. He was very excited. It was a great assignment for me, as I had never done an album cover before. The other plus was that it was a documentary type of assignment, which is, stylistically, how I like to shoot. It was a strange situation, though, since the art director had already hired another photographer for the job. Jeff had called me on a Friday and the shoot was the following Monday. We ran up to Sony together so I could show them some of my work. Jeff then took me on a whirlwind tour around the company, introduced me to the people who worked for him, and stuffed a bunch of CDs in my bag. He took little cards he had made with my pictures on them announcing his shows and stuck them all over the walls at Sony and gave them to people. Then he took me with him to Howard Wuelfing's office so he could get some advice on a publicity imaging problem that needed some work. *Then* we popped into a cab and sped down to his house, where he made me watch him call up the other photographer and unhire her for the job. The tornado that was Jeff.

I think what amazes me now is how he fought for me to photograph his first project. As I said, I had not shot album covers before, and nobody knew who I was at Sony. He knew I was the one for the job and insisted that it happened. I will never forget that; it opened doors for me creatively and professionally, and I believe that is because he trusted me and had faith in my work. I loved him for that. He was an amazingly talented performer and had the ability to recognize the creative potential in other people, a catalyst for other artists. You wanted to meet his talent with the best of yourself. In this regard he was truly inspiring.

The day of the Sin-é shoot, it was overcast and a bit drizzly. During the morning and early afternoon the technicians were getting the recording gear set up and people were walking in and out of the café wondering what was up. They were going to record two full sets that day: one in the late afternoon, one at night. It was very tense, with everybody waiting around. The business guys and people from the company built up a really pressurized atmosphere; he knew a lot was expected of him. It conjured an intensely protective and somewhat maternal feeling in me. Here he was, this big goofy kid all jazzed up, scared and still unjaded to the big business of art and commerce. In the afternoon we went into Tompkins Square Park for a while to take some shots outside and get a bit of air. It was raining lightly, but it was beautiful light for photos; the puddles and water dripping seemed suited to him. He preferred it. His vulnerability comes out in the pictures from that time. He had his Scorpionic darkness and lightning bolt wit, but as soon as his fingers hit the strings, there emerged this open, loving energy that stilled every chattering voice in the room. Jeff walked onto the stage slowly, quietly clapping out a beat, and began his rendition of Nina Simone's song "Be My Husband," a cappella.

A lot of the shots of him warming up are pretty funny, because he had a lot of steam to blow off. During that time I climbed up on the ladder and took the shot that ended up on the cover. I liked that shot because it was totally real. He was warming up in the corner and everyone sitting in the café was doing their own thing; the guy reading the paper was too funny. I think Jeff's choice for the cover reflected that on some level. He just viewed himself as this regular dude and wasn't really adjusted to all of the hoopla and hype yet. It reminds me of a conversation we were having during the middle of the *Grace* shoot where he was going on about how he was just this regular guy. I was shooting and am tremendously non-verbal when I'm in that visual state, but he got me laughing till my belly hurt. He just kept giving me that wide-eyed look, working the moment like an expert comedian. At times he would frustrate me by getting into some intense subjects or feelings when we were shooting and I would be in this visual world where I could hear him but not fully respond because I was working. I feel that my role with him was as a sort of witness; a friend, but witness also. I think of later on when I knew him better and we were on the road and I was photographing all the time. We would be somewhere in a room of people and he would look

around till he caught my eye, to see that I was watching. He might smile and continue what he was doing. I don't think it was vanity, I think he just liked feeling he was being looked after.

Anyway, I'm drifting. Back to Sin-é.

After the first set was over, Jeff seemed overwhelmed. We went to the other side of Sin-é where the bar was and he seemed like he was about to collapse. He draped himself across some chairs, put his head on my lap, and passed out. During the second set of the evening he was warmed up and a little more relaxed. His friends started coming by, Hal Willner, Rebecca Moore, Brenda Kahn, Nick Hill, and many more, and the place got really packed. A fabulous recording debut.

For the *Grace* album-cover shoot I asked my friend Billy Basinski if we could use his amazing loft Arcadia, in Williamsburg, Brooklyn, to do the photographs. The space was very opulent and textural and I used some of the surfaces as they were and also built some sets to shoot against. It was once again a sort of high-pressure situation for Jeff and he was pretty nervous coming in, knowing that a lot was expected from him. There were quite a few business people there watching, so part of my job was to distract him from feeling self-conscious and ease him into the moment. Of course it is easier to photograph people on a one-to-one basis, but when that's not possible it is important to create a relaxed space in whatever way you can conjure so people lose their self-consciousness. With Jeff we started on a black backdrop to warm up and let him jump around to throw off some of the nervousness. Then he did what came naturally and started writing in his notebook, sitting under the table with clocks all over it. As things warmed up images started evolving, the atmosphere lightened, and we started to experiment. The amazing thing about photographing Jeff was his willingness to try almost any idea I put forward. Being able to create photos with him was a unique experience because of his creative and playful energy, and his trust. He did not try to censor or control while we were doing the work; he was willing to meet me, follow a lead, and be present. Even when he wasn't totally in love with an idea.

I think it is important to point out that there are not that many typically considered "beautiful people" who are really very interesting to photograph. Jeff had a fantastic beauty, rare and originating on an energetic level. It's got nothing to do with the meat of a body, and it's beyond talent. Maybe his high burn rate made him shine all the more brightly, seducing people to match an ephemeral brilliance, or by the same token a vast darkness. Whatever you might call it, it became an actual and visible expression in the photographs. They are a mixture really, half reflection and half projection, recombining in different proportions in every picture. He was, on a creative level, totally open, beautiful.

Later, in the winter of '94, Jeff invited me to go on the road with him for a couple of weeks to photograph him and his band on tour. It was an amazing opportunity to shoot the band because it enabled me to reflect an authentic picture of day-to-day life on the road. It took a few days for the guys in the band to get used to me slinking around with my camera everywhere, but I think because Jeff was so accepting of the situation they were willing to open up as well. It was an amazing experience and I felt warmly adopted into their road family, feeling like I had a bunch of new brothers, Michael Tighe, Matt Johnson, and Mick Grondahl, with Gene Bowen, Jeff's tour manager, as mother of the motley crew. Every morning Gene would come around with Xeroxes of the day's upcoming events. I got my own bunk and quickly settled into the smelliness of life on the bus and the great unwashed. In the few weeks I was with them, we traveled throughout Texas, Louisiana, and Florida. It was a disconcerting way to live, waking up in strange parking lots and not really knowing what state you were in sometimes, and even though I only tasted it for a short while, it is a different and insular reality where the crew is your family and the bus is your home. Sort of like a rocket ship flying through space landing on different unknown planets. The schedule of the days varied, but the afternoons were usually made up of Jeff juggling a number of interviews and then doing in-store performances and radio shows with the band. Then there would be a load-in, a sound check, some strange-looking food for dinner, and then that evening's performance. The band would usually be up till the wee hours, the bus would be loaded up, and then we would pile into it headed for the next venue. Sometimes, when there was an extra day between shows, we would be booked into a hotel with some clean sheets, a shower, and a washing machine. Hallelujah.

In terms of shooting, I had my cameras on all of the time. It became a part of my anatomy and the guys got used to it as I integrated into the daily life and became part of the crew. It was a wonderful experience, and I feel very privileged that they so openly accepted me as a part of their road family.

Besides the shoots I have mentioned I photographed Jeff a number of other times on my own, and sometimes when he played around in New York. I was able to photograph him over the course of five years and record some of his life and development as an artist. Some people have asked me why it is that I went back and photographed him so much, and I think there are a number of reasons. One is the obvious: that he was a great and talented musician. But beyond that, I feel that through the work we developed a meaningful friendship that was based on trust and mutual respect for the work we did. He opened up and allowed me into his space in a way that I haven't explored to that level with anyone else. His desire to become and claim his own authentic self, I think, reflects back in many of the images, and the fact that he allowed me to stand witness is a gift I will never forget.

I want to thank everyone who participated in the making of this book. I know that Jeff's passing still seems shocking and hard to make sense of. I thank the people who talked with me and helped me create this portrait. I hope this book gives the people that knew him some comfort and others that know him through his music a sense of who he was as a human being. The making of this book has for me been a process of healing and forgiveness and was made with much love and the hope that it can be of use to others as well. Jeff affected and changed everyone he came into contact with, whether it was one-on-one or through his amazing voice. The way he influenced people, challenged us in a way to come into contact with our own true selves, is something that has certainly stimulated me to become myself, truthfully, and evolve into and through some of my deepest fears. He was my friend and teacher. He will truly live on through the ways he has influenced us, our memories, and the love we carry for him in our hearts. Inshallah.

A special thanks and love to Cory Cyr and Jim Stoeri. I couldn't have made this book without you.

—*Merri Cyr*

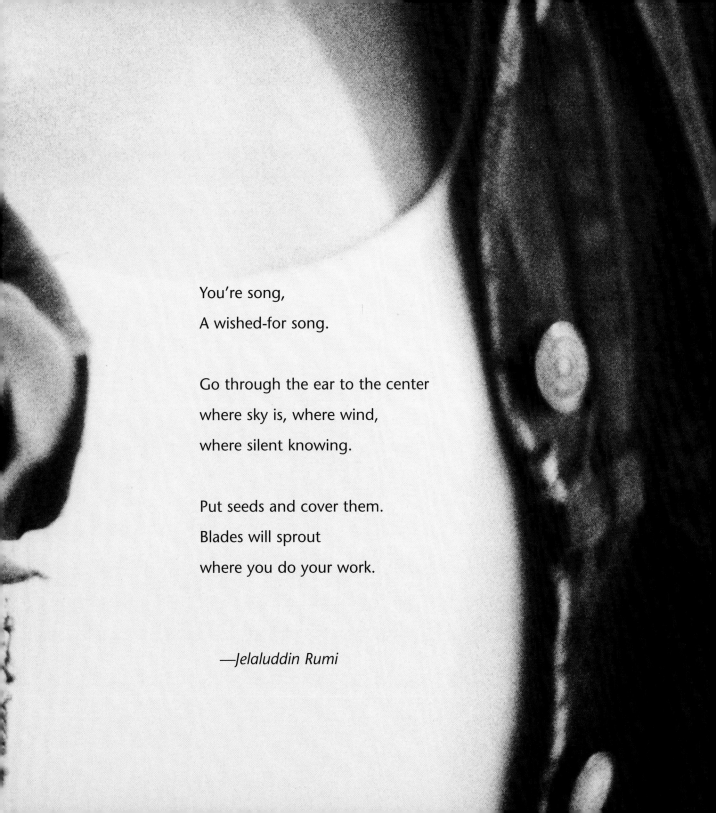

You're song,
A wished-for song.

Go through the ear to the center
where sky is, where wind,
where silent knowing.

Put seeds and cover them.
Blades will sprout
where you do your work.

—*Jelaluddin Rumi*

Steve Berkowitz sent a note around to a few people at Columbia, saying that he was trying to sign this guy, Jeff Buckley, who was playing at Sin-é. I had never been there before. It was this really teeny cramped room on the Lower East Side. It was the middle of the summer, and this guy with this little buzz haircut and green military pants with suspenders was standing in the middle of the "stage."

I thought, "Who is this punk? What attitude!" By the end of the first song, I was so overwhelmed with what I was hearing that I forgot about everything in the world for two hours.

I was hooked.

—*Leah Reid*

Late one afternoon, I get a call: "We need to set up a trade shot with a new signing, Jeff Buckley—right now! Find us a photographer."

After some frantic begging phone calls, I get a photographer to show up. I take him downstairs to the A&R department and gather the executives together for the shot: the president of the label, Don Ienner, the business affairs guy, Steve Berkowitz from A&R and such. Now they're all together and I ask Steve, "So where's your artist?" "I don't know," he replies. I comb the A&R offices and everyone's *seen* this Buckley kid but no one knows where he's gone off to. I look back in on the executives and they're getting restless.

I start checking the rest of the floor, room by room. I reach the "special products" division and there's Jeff. He ferreted out one exec who still played in local bands and here they are happily chatting about mutual musician friends, recent gigs, incredibly obscure old records. Jeff's totally oblivious to this little matter of his first official record company trade shot. And that's how I first met Jeff.

A year later, Jeff saunters into my office with a mock-up of the cover of Live at Sin-é. "Do I look too cute here?" We corral a young lady, show her the artwork and she's delighted: "You look great! Just like Luke Perry!" With that, Jeff gives a theatrical YELP and bolts down the hall, Wile E. Coyote style.

—*Howard Wuelfing*

It was a couple months before Hal Willner did the Tim Buckley tribute at St. Anne's. Hal and I had already known each other a long time and we were working on a Charles Mingus tribute record at Columbia. Hal, at that time lived on the other side of Tompkins Square Park on Avenue B, and we would meet up there and hang out, or be at the studio and walk down St. Marks Place across Tompkins Square Park to go over to his place to listen to the recordings that we'd been working on. A couple of months before the Tim Buckley tribute, he asked, "I'm looking for a certain Tim Buckley record, do you have any of them?" As it happened, I did, and I loaned it to Hal. One of the days when we were walking along St. Marks Place, he said, "I think his kid is coming." That was the first time that I ever knew that there was a kid, and that this kid was Jeff Buckley. And I asked, "Oh. What's he gonna do?" Hal said, "Well, I guess he sings. I don't really know, I never really heard him." As it turns out I didn't go to the Tim Buckley tribute but some people told me, "We went to the Buckley tribute and his kid was amazing." I said, "Oh?" They said, "He sounded just like him." End that part of the story . . .

We're walking across St. Marks Place one day many months later and Hal says, "Hey! Buckley's kid is playing in here!" (the newly opened Sin-é). It was a cool evening and we needed a cup of coffee and we went in. In the corner of the room there's a little ragamuffin of a guy, and I said, "Hey, that's Jeff Buckley, okay." There's about five people in there . . . there's no scene, there was no following, in fact it was sort of before he was even really Jeff Buckley. He was still in Gods and Monsters with Gary Lucas. He was halfway through one song and my jaw just dropped. "Hal, what the fuck's going on here? Listen to this guy!" He said, "Yeah, he's good." He had been in this band and he was just the singer, he wasn't even playing guitar in Gods and Monsters. So he would show up at Sin-é and just kind of play songs he thought of. This was the beginning. We talked immediately, he knew and liked Hal and I was introduced as a person who knew something about music. Jeff and I just kind of hit it off immediately, just as people and music lovers. So we went on from there.

The street scene down on St. Marks was pretty wild 'cause Jeff went from playing to Tree Man (a homeless guy) and nobodies to limos and playing for the chairmen of all these record companies practically on the same night. Jeff would look at me and go, "How does this work?" I said, "This is what happens when someone becomes the IT. You're the IT."

—*Steve Berkowitz*

He was very secure as an artist. He didn't doubt his talent. He never talked about it because it was like some people having blue eyes. He just had it. It was most evident when he played at Sin-é. I felt very maternal to him, right from the beginning. The first time he played here twelve people and the club manager (who at the time was a guy named Max) came. When Jeff went on, I was upstairs in the office when Max came running upstairs and said, "Who is this guy? He is a genius!" Jeff didn't care if there was nobody in the room, he was giving the show everything. I said, "Well, when he's done I want you to give him dinner and make sure that he gets paid." That's how I felt about him. He came in here a lot to eat. He didn't come in here just because we gave him free food, he just came because he knew if I was here I was going to sit down and talk to him and if I wasn't, he could just be anony-

mous and have his meal. He was very wanted here. It really makes me cry, because I know how he felt and I felt so . . . pleased that we could give that to him and I really feel that was more important than giving him a stage to play on because he could get that anywhere. On his birthday in November of 1993, I called from India and I said, "I want a birthday cake on the stage," and they made a beautiful cake for him. I wasn't there to see it, but I heard about it. I just didn't want him to think that the person that he was was not important, the person was more important. If he never sang another day in his life it would be everybody's loss, but he was so . . . important. For some reason I think he wasn't sure about that, he knew that he had the gift, but I'm not sure that he knew that if he didn't have the gift, that he was still okay, that he was of great value anyway. Everybody in here knew what he want-ed, he'd come in and he'd have the frittata of the day and eighty thousand cups of coffee, and everyone loved him. Loved him.

—*Ellen Cavolina*

We prepared a deal ourselves, a proposal we gave to all the record companies saying, "This is what we're looking for." And then when everybody said that's acceptable, it just became as it should be, which was the best record company on an artistic level. Why Columbia? For a couple of reasons. One, they were there early. Steve Berkowitz was one of the first on the scene. He was there very early on at the shows, and he and Jeff were connecting. At the top, Donnie Ienner was saying the right things. When I would have my discussions with him I'd impress upon him that we had to have time to put together a band and to write. We'd have to have full creative control. And he just said yes yes yes yes yes. So we were satisfied on that creative level. Finally, the history of Columbia Records: that was the label of Bob Dylan. They gave him creative support, they supported him in terms of resources, enabling him travel all over the world. Right off the bat. Very unusual for new artists. From the get-go Jeff was given absolute artistic priority. Columbia felt that it was a long-term project. He was really worried about being chewed up by the large corporation and going into the belly of the beast. He had enough character to say at one point, "Well, maybe this is going too fast. Do I have to actually do it?" That was very Jeff. My recommendation was that this was his time. I knew the record business, and music and fashion are fickle. I felt that this was his moment to strike, but do it on his terms.

—George Stein

Columbia knew about him because of Tim Buckley's memorial. It started coming down, and then quickly people knew about Jeff Buckley. He was playing every week at Sin-é and that sort of kicked in. Jeff would do two- or three-hour marathons. There was big word of mouth. Soon Jeff had record label presidents coming down to see him. There was one famous show where Clive Davis was in one corner, Donnie Ienner in another corner, Seymour Stein in another corner. And Jeff didn't have a tape and he was only doing covers. It ran counter to industry wisdom, which is that you have to be doing originals. And one night he'd do blues and another night he'd do rock 'n' roll, another night he might do folk stuff or another night he'd mix it up. He was always experimenting. Sometimes he'd do Pakistani cover songs by Nusrat Fateh Ali Khan. Donnie Ienner said to me, "I don't know what this kid is, I can't pigeonhole him." But he was a great talent and he wanted him.

—*George Stein*

When I first saw him, I saw the T-shirt and the pants hanging off his ass . . . and that chain. I came from more of a rock background and I thought I had to change his image. I said, "We gotta do something about these chains and these pants and this fucking T-shirt and everything." That's when I didn't understand Jeff yet. And I must sound like a real idiot when I even talk about that stuff. He made allowances I think for me at the beginning. I think he saw through it. He knew my heart was in the right place. The biggest line we had was, we always said, "It's about the music, stupid." That's really the key . . . That could be the title of a book. If I ever wrote a book, it would start off "It's about the music, stupid."

—Dave Lory

I realized that he got signed to the label and there were no songs, there was no tape . . . which is unheard of for how people get signed. It was all pretty clear that this was an incredibly gifted person.

—Steve Berkowitz

I think I was very lucky. I think he always trusted me and I'm very proud to be able to say that. And I think he always knew I was there to protect him and to look after him and not to exploit him. Although my brief was to promote an artist it was more sort of artist relations, to make sure that the artist was happy. And I did, I felt very maternal toward him, as anybody would with Jeff. I think he brought out that quality, he was so likable and so innocent, for want of a better word. I took it very seriously. That was another quality about Jeff: he would bring out this thing in people where you wanted to please him. That was why so many people put so much care into what they did around him. Because he deserved it, he did what he did so well that you couldn't let him down.

—Sam Way

One of the things that fascinated Jeff about me was something that he had never considered before, that someone could be a powerfu artist and have a career without being a part of the industry.

When he met Rebecca Moore, who introduced him to me, he started finding out about the whole downtown arts scene. Coming from Anaheim, California, that Disney box he escaped from, and from L.A., the East Village and downtown New York was a whole other world, and he was fascinated by the artists who made up that world. Jeff loved the idea that as an artist you are the continuatior of an artistic history. He was starting to build this world that was so different from the bleak L.A. world that he described to me, or of the rock world in general, which was being around a lot of single-minded and competitive people who could only see three months into the future and the possibility of getting a record contract.

Jeff was turned on to a lot of people that he never heard of and he was exposed to epic thinkers, people who have real lives. Artists who go to see other artists' work, not to network but to actually see the work. Jeff was very drawn to this idea of an artistic life. The idea of cross-fertilization was fantastic to him and suited him. Jeff was both a very improvisational person as well as a methodical per-son who worked at acquiring skills. The whole period of his life from about 1992 to 1997, which was about five years, was this enor-mous personal odyssey in which Jeff opened himself up, re-nurtured and reinvented himself.

—Penny Arcade

I went to Philadelphia to see Jeff play at the Grape

Street Pub. Before the show I showed him six or

eight possible album covers, and he was immedi-

ately drawn to the particular photo that was even-

tually chosen. That photo meant so much to

him—not because of what he was wearing, or

how he looked, but because he could tell by the

expression on his face that he was listening to

music while the photo was being taken. That was

so important to him. It wasn't about anything else

but the MUSIC, and he wanted the album cover to

represent that.

—*Leah Reid*

We didn't do movie soundtracks because we didn't want Jeff to break on a soundtrack. He wanted to break on doing his own thing. He turned down some major acting roles too. Jeff Buckley was supposed to be the student in *The Mirror Has Two Faces*. He got offered that role and that was one of many.

He turned down a lot of money to write the theme song for a Quentin Tarantino film. We would bring it to him, and we'd explain the pros and cons to each decision. I mean, we'd offer our opinions but it got to the point where I pretty much knew what he would or wouldn't do. But I always brought things to him, I never made any decisions for him.

I miss protecting him. I think that's probably the hardest thing. I've never said that or thought about it, but it was protecting him and protecting his music and bringing him across the way he wanted to be brought across. That's the joy of it. Forget the money, forget all the other bullshit, because at the end of the day when you walk in the door and you see him, you see that you've protected his baby. And that's his art. And him personally.

—Dave Lory

When Jeff loved people, he loved them unconditionally. Whether others thought that someone was a big freak or the best person in the world, it didn't make any difference to him. He loved people for what they were, unconditionally. However, he wasn't the kind of person that someone could pursue any sort of friendship with; it usually had to be on his terms. He said that he was like a cat. "When come around—it's going to be often, but it's going to be when I want." That was fine by me. I always made time for him. He was very catlike, and everything about him was very feline.

—*Leah Rei*

e was such a true artist. Such a student of his art. So inspired by the work that he was throwing himself into, and I suppose tortured y it too but it was a really beautiful thing to watch. Watching somebody work that hard, in public, is pretty wonderful. He was such a enerous spirit. I've never been inspired by an artist quite that much, before or since. Not to that level.

—*Nicholas Hill*

en I started working with Jeff, I asked him
ut his early influences and he shocked me
onding, "The two most important
rds to me growing up were George
in's *AM/FM* and Led Zeppelin's *Physical
ffiti*." This is not what I expected! "When
as a kid, I learned George Carlin's routines
heart," he recounted. "When my mom
w parties, I'd do them for the guests."

s later, performing solo at Fez or Sin-é,
could always count on Jeff following a
rtbreakingly beautiful reading of "La Vie
Rose" or "Strange Fruit" with an outbreak
heesy jokes or spot on impressions of any-
from cartoon characters like Bugs Bunny
musical icons such as Nina Simone.

dad was an auto mechanic," he
ained, "but he was a music freak." Every
day he'd bring home a stack of new
ums and play them for us." The first LP
pecifically bought for Jeff was *Physical
ffiti*, kindling a love for Zep that remained
him throughout his life. Only Jeff
ght Plant's occasional hints at Arabic
ence to full blossom drawing on the
ence of the great Pakistani Qawwali
er Nusrat Fateh Ali Khan.

often said, "Nusrat is my Elvis."

—*Howard Wuelfing*

If all anyone knew of him was the record, they'd just think he was this intense, moody sort of person. But if they had a chance to see him live, they would see glimpses of what he was really about. He loved to laugh and make people laugh. His sense of humor really balanced off the intensity. He said that his "sign" was Beavis, with Butthead Rising.

—Leah Reid

I think it was in '93 that Jeff came to our house for Christmas. My wife, our two young boys, and Jeff. He shows up a couple of hours late in the afternoon wearing a top hat and a fur coat. It was the first appearance of the fur coat; he had just purchased it. I think he had just gotten some money from Sony. He bought a top hat and this fur coat. I think the left sleeve was held together by safety pins. He appeared at our front door.

Our sons Nick and Ben were one and three years old at this time. No record had come out yet. He was leaving later that day to England to visit people, visit some friends. He showed up at our house carrying an open, half-used Christmas basket which he had gotten for a gift from Columbia Records. This was his offering to the Christmas festivities at our house that day. There was a Christmas tree and he put the open basket, with half of the stuff in it eaten, under the Christmas tree, which I thought was really nice. He was sharing his booty. And I thought that was very sweet. That was just a great day, a lot of lying on the floor playing with the kids. He exhibited something that day which I had never seen before. It's late in the afternoon, now the television is on and Warner Brothers' Looney Tunes and Merrie Melodies cartoons were on and my three-year-old son was sitting on the couch. All of a sudden Jeff got up and stood next to the television, just to the side of it. He was word-for-word miming these cartoons, and these are some maniacal music and maniacal songs with extremely complicated rhythms to the soundtracks and the pratfalls. He knew every beat and every word. My son Nick, who always spoke very well, he kept looking at Jeff and looking at the TV and looking at me, and this went on for a couple of minutes and Nick finally went, "Dad, how is he doing that?!" And I said, "I don't know, Nick. I don't know . . . Just sit down and watch him."

—*Steve Berkowitz*

When we'd go to Al Green's church he'd dress up. I remember the last time we went to church, I had some friends from Washington in town and we went to pick him up. I got to his house and he wasn't ready. He was talking to his aunt on his father's side. And he had his green toe-nails and his suit and suspenders, and a belt I think. And his fly was undone. I said, "Jeff, zip your pants up."

—*Andria Lisle*

I remember when I got pregnant and I hadn't seen him in a while 'cause he was on the road and he came in one day and my stomach was bulging and he was jumping up and down— "Is there a baby in there?" He was freaking out. He imme-diately got on his hands and knees and started singing to my stomach. It was so incredible. He said "Baby, if you can hear me . . ." and I told him the baby's name. He was singing to her . . .

—*Ellen Cavolina*

I really pissed him off once, it's really funny. He was on his way to England or France, probably England, to pick up or present some award . . . I believe he was presenting an award to Jimmy Page for something. We were going to the airport, I was taking him to the Concorde and I made a tape for him the night before, a Led Zeppelin tape, this really cool live Zeppelin. I swear, I remember putting the headphones on his head and he just mimicked all of the air guitar and air drum parts, he knew all of the "live" idiosyncasies of the Zeppelin show. So we were groovin' to that, and we get to the airport and he has one little bag and we get to the counter and some really stuffy lady that did the ticketing says, "Oh, Jeff Buckley. What are you, a musician or something?" He responds, "Yeah, I'm a musician." [laugh] And she counters, "What kind of music do you play, how do you describe your music?"

The age-old question for Jeff, right? And he didn't know. He just said "umm," and he looked at me. I quipped, "Triple A" [chuckle], which is this old adult rock-folk alternative format. Jeff got really pissed off. [laugh] He shot back some expletives like "Fuck you, you dick." In a half-joking way I said it and he half-jokingly got back at me. He wasn't able to describe his music. I was kind of reminding him; I wouldn't try to be cruel to him, but I was reminding him of some current realities, because with "Last Goodbye" a hit on MTV and radio, I think he liked that. He liked the idea of his music getting widely heard. He talked about his different sides: how he could be on a "rock star trip" with some, but also be a "buddy on the road" like he was with me. I'll always remember that look, he looked at me like . . . what!?

—Jack Bookbinder

He had very good instincts. He'd reject nine out of ten offers, things that'd make him a lot of money. Like the Prada shoot, things like that, and movie roles like *The Mirror Has Two Faces*. "Look, I'm a musician," is what he'd say. "I'm not an actor, I'm not a model, why do I have to waste time on that, that's gonna get in the way of my real important purpose in life, music. Music for the people."

—*Jack Bookbinder*

I was watching this old videotape that someone showed me of Jeff playing when he was in this garage band in high school. He looked about fifteen years old and those guys were playing songs by Rush, Styx, Genesis, and Queen. He already had all the moves he used later in his career down, except that his voice was a few octaves higher at that point . . .

—*Merri Cyr*

He went in to an Arista Records meeting and he showed up late. I waited for him in the reception area and he comes wandering in with a ripped T-shirt, his old flea-market pants, and a see-through plastic bag containing Ajax and bathroom cleaner and he just carried that to the meeting with him. This meeting was with the president of the company.

—*George Stein*

"What is it you women have in here?" Anyway, that was the time he sat me down and was like, "You gotta remember there are boys and there are men, Dave is a boy." That night I was sort of wandering around and he took his hat and put it on my head and said, "This is the happy hat. This is going to make you happy. You gotta hold onto it until you feel better." So that became a little bit of a joke.

When Dave actually proposed to me onstage at Arlene Grocery, I remember, after getting dragged up onstage and Dave did this big proposal in front of everyone, Dave said, "Okay, Jeff. Am I a man now?" And Jeff said, "Yup, you're a man."

—Sam Way

Either I grabbed Dave's hand or he grabbed mine; we had a little moment. Then I looked back and I saw Jeff with this smirk on his face. I tried to go into denial and pretend that Jeff hadn't seen anything, but I'm sure that that was the point that he knew. Then I think about little moments after that and he played with us. He really played with us.

I remember one time in Paris when Dave and I had had a blazing row. I was really upset. Jeff, bless him, because we were friends, he was just protective of me. He came to my hotel room for a shower. He's like, "I need to have a shower" and I was like, "Wow. Jeff hasn't had a shower in weeks." And he started going through my whole vanity bag or whatever and pulling out my bust-firming cream and God knows what, and really ripping me about that.

It was the day we were doing the album-cover shoot in Brooklyn. I heard Jeff tell Merri, "I'll be your muse. I want you to take pictures of me forever and ever." He just loved the vibe that he had with her, and that just set the stage for the relationship that those two were going to have. Now, whenever I see one of her pictures, I always think, "Yeah, he definitely was her muse. And vice versa."

—*Leah Reid*

I was worried that he'd believe the hype. There were so many people telling him that he was the greatest thing on earth. Sometimes I'd see him get real quiet and introverted. I remembered the story about when Julius Caesar entered the Roman forum; they'd go "Hail Caesar!," acting like he was a god. This is a story about a Roman tradition. A slave would whisper into the emperor's ear, "You are only a man, you are only a man." And I told him that story. I said, "Just remember who you are, I know that you have the strength of character." *New York* magazine wanted to do a cover story about Jeff, New York's next big thing. He was really upset because he felt, "What have I done to deserve this?" He felt he hadn't done anything yet and that his reputation was getting ahead of itself. Why did he have this big reputation? It's because people saw the talent. But he wasn't convinced because he hadn't sold any records yet. He was getting uptight about that.

His death was so hard to believe because he was so godlike in his talents. You couldn't believe his life could be snuffed out. That he was mortal. His talent was so immortal. And to get those two in the same body and soul was a dichotomy. He was so vulnerable with a lot of baggage and problems to work out and at the same time he had this ascendance, talent beyond even him. Maybe he was even grappling with that. A perfect talent in a human being who was flawed like all of us. There was a tendency to think, well, if the talent's perfect, then Jeff has to be completely perfect and together. The expectations that were on him for the next record or the next song. Everybody probably had more confidence in him than he did. But he was the one that had to be up late at night alone with his insecurities.

—*George Stein*

I was getting a lot of offers to go to labels over the last couple of years. None of them I took seriously. I guess it got down on the street in the Village, and Jeff showed up one day . . . Mercury had made me an offer. Jeff cared but he wouldn't show it until the last minute. He came to the office one day and he's there for about six or eight hours reading fan mail. And he kept opening fan mail and everybody was going, "Why is Jeff hanging out here all fucking day?" It took Jeff six or eight hours before he finally could . . . I went out on the balcony of my office to have a cigarette. It took him forever to get around to the question. The question was, "So, I hear you might be going to a label?" And I said, "Well, I've had offers. Does that bother you?" He says, "Yeah. You're my guy." And I said, "So I matter?" He said, "Yeah." "Well, I'm not going anywhere." We had the hugs and then we went on with life.

He's had a tremendous effect on the music industry.

The thing that's amazing is I get tapes all the time that say, "Oh, it sounds like Buckley." Everybody wants to be like him, but nobody ever will. Just like nobody else will ever be another Dylan or Patti Smith. When I look at artists now I just have a totally different feeling for what I see. He was special. You can't describe Jeff Buckley. Nobody can write a book about Jeff Buckley. Nobody can put Jeff Buckley in a bottle and say this is what it is. Jeff was from the heart and the soul. There's very few. I really believe Jeff was the future of rock 'n' roll. I think Jeff made a difference. We used to laugh and say, "If you're having problems with your woman, you just give them a Jeff Buckley CD and say, 'Baby, this is what I'm trying to say.'"

He just had a big heart, he always cared about everybody. He'd come up and play with my daughter. He had a real love for my wife [Sam Way] and my daughter. And he really cared about people that were around him. If you were having a bad day, he would care.

—Dave Lory

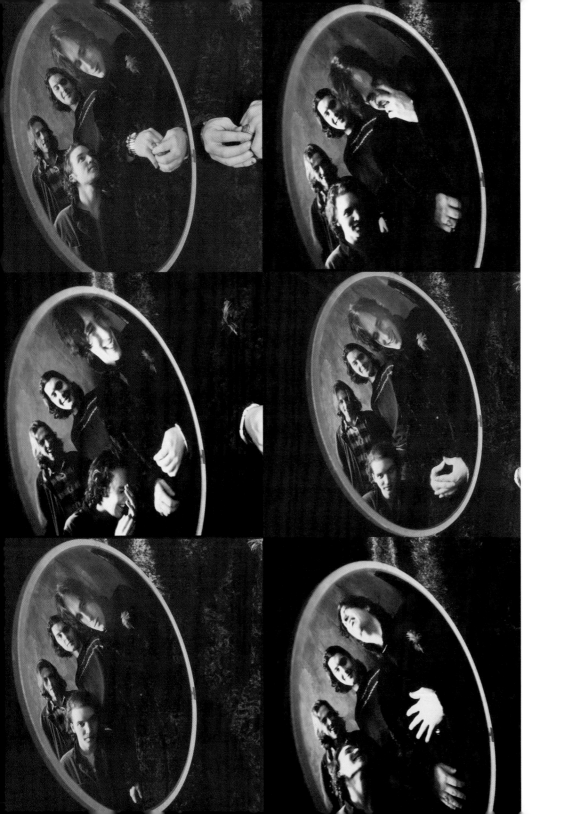

I never met anybody like Jeff Buckley before. The feeling from the moment I saw him that first time at Sin-é, like that silly pasta commercial, I said, "Hal, it's all in there, isn't it? It's just all in there." from him bouncing around from a Billie Holiday to a Judy Garland to a Bad Brains to goofing on Geddy Lee to bouncing back and doing a Sly or Curtis Mayfield to Hank Williams to Robert Johnson, it's like, what kind of fucking childhood did this guy have? This is a guy who spent a lot of time in his room. And his ability to play the guitar and phrase very large soundscapes in a very minimal way was truly unique. His ideas in arranging, just in the way he inverted his chords, and the spacing between the chords and the rhythm that he used on even known changes of cover songs he would do, were uniquely him.

—*Steve Berkowitz*

I was there [Shangri-la Records] and he would come in at the end of the day and wait for me to get out of work and walk the dog and stuff. He'd come in and trade CDs for other CDs. And he really liked to come in and just be funny, impersonating all the customers. No one would know who he was. I mean it was always inevitable that someone would come in and start talking about Jeff Buckley being in town and Jeff would be parodying them.

There was a Vietnamese restaurant called Saigon Le, and he had a bike and he ate at Saigon Le all the time. He ate there so much that they gave him a Saigon Le shirt. So there was a rumor going around that he was their delivery boy, because he would be seriously pedaling his bike all around midtown.

He was such a sweet baby, you know? And it was funny 'cause my roommate and I really started listening to his music in earnest. You'd get to the point where you'd be embarrassed because he'd be knocking on the door and *Grace* would be blasting. I never talked to him about his music or asked him about it. I feel if I liked something so much then I really don't have to say anything about it, you know what I mean? I wish I had told him. I mean, he knew. I remember playing a Captain Beefheart record for him and being like damn, you should do this song. I had no idea about him and Gary Lucas, I mean that's how ignorant I was. Even though I worked in a record store I didn't know anything about Jeff's history. I knew who his father was, that's about it. Sometimes I would go out and I would hear other people talk about him in this completely different vein. Like, "Oh, I heard Jeff Buckley's going to be at this bar tonight," which was weird, because he was somebody that I walked my dog with.

—Andria Lisle

"The Sky Is a Landfill" is an incredibly political song. It's about tearing down what separates you from reality, the natural world. When he played that song for me I flipped out.

Jeff was intrigued by my partner, Al Giordano, who was both a music writer and a super-radical political reporter from the *Boston Phoenix*. Al had written a manifesto called "The Media Is the Middleman" that Jeff loved, which was based on concepts from my show *Love, Sex and Sanity*. "The Sky Is a Landfill" is directly connected with that thinking and with the artist Jack Smith, whose ideas Jeff loved especially; they deal with the question of whether art can ever be useful.

Jeff was an exceptionally smart person and a natural intellectual. A true thinker. I think what started to make him unhappy and depressed was he went from being a guy who was improvising, entertaining the audience with physical comedy, pulling it all out of thin air, the guy who learned Nusrat Fateh Ali Khan's "Hulka-Hulka" by heart, who was a human jukebox at Sin-é, to being a guy who goes on tour and only plays the ten songs on his album.

—*Penny Arcade*

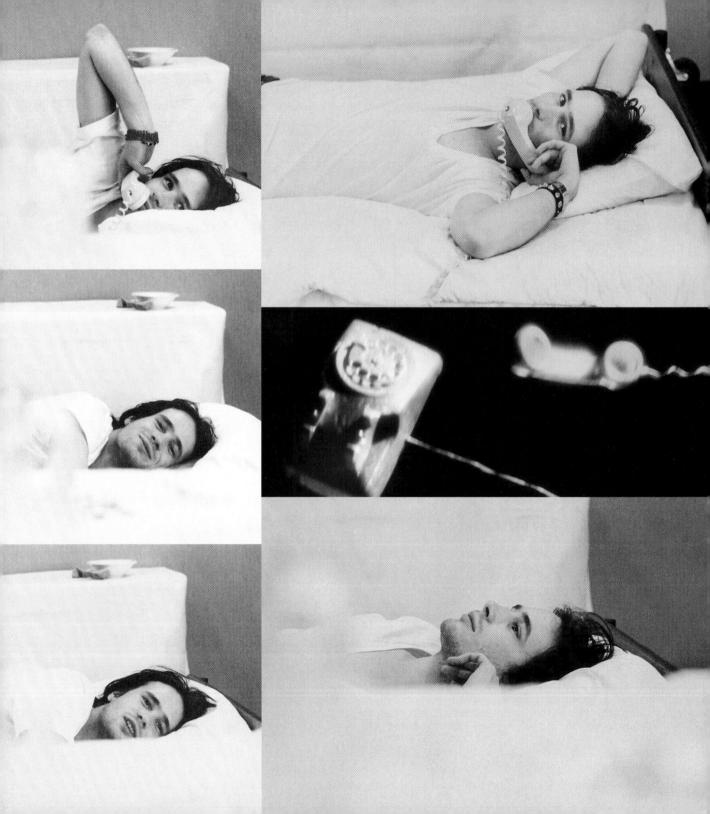

He was capable of being a rock star, capable of dealing with the press. But it wasn't healthy for him; it didn't make him happy. At the same time he was saying that he wanted to maintain his indie credibility, he's signing with the biggest label in the world. Again, that's another representation of his dualistic nature. He tried to have it both ways.

—Nicholas Hill

Mainly the work Jeff and I did together was TV or radio interviews in hotel rooms. Jeff was incredibly hardworking. I found that he was very open with people, very trusting. He had a lack of confidence in some ways, because he didn't want to do the wrong thing. There was no act, it was all him. His interviews were just very natural, no pretense about them. I remember one day we flew out of Paris in the morning . . . Jeff, Dave, and I. We went straight to a hotel in Frankfurt and he was literally locked into a hotel room and he churned out about, I don't know, fourteen interviews. Radio interviews on the trot. We flew back the same day, straight into Paris again. He was very professional. I've seen artists get pissed off and get snarky or whatever, but he treated everybody with respect.

—Sam Way

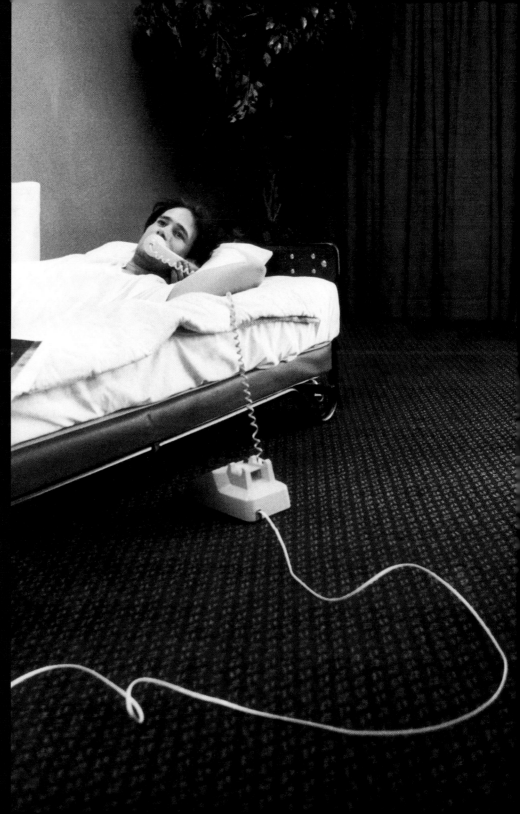

Everything was improvisational. There were song structures, when he had a band he had to some degree stay within those structures, but when he played by himself he could be completely free to have everything go on its own journey. He was a jazz musician in that he played from the heart. He had massive technique and a pool of possibilities to draw from melodically, rhythmically, lyrically. It was endless, sort of like Sonny Rollins, he could play everything. He could play everything all within the same song. Jeff

could do that. One night, I saw him do "Strange Fruit" at a club, someplace on First Ave. and First. He was gonna play a middle set at CBGB's, solo, two hours later. He played "Strange Fruit" again, but he played it in a minor key and with slide. It was just radically and completely different, and they both worked! The next night I saw him and he played it in a different key again, not in an open tuning. He played what he felt, he played like what he was, he played the mood that he was in. In some ways he was a jazz musician and a performance artist, he would much rather have probably always done something different every day, if he was in the mood for that.

—*Steve Berkowitz*

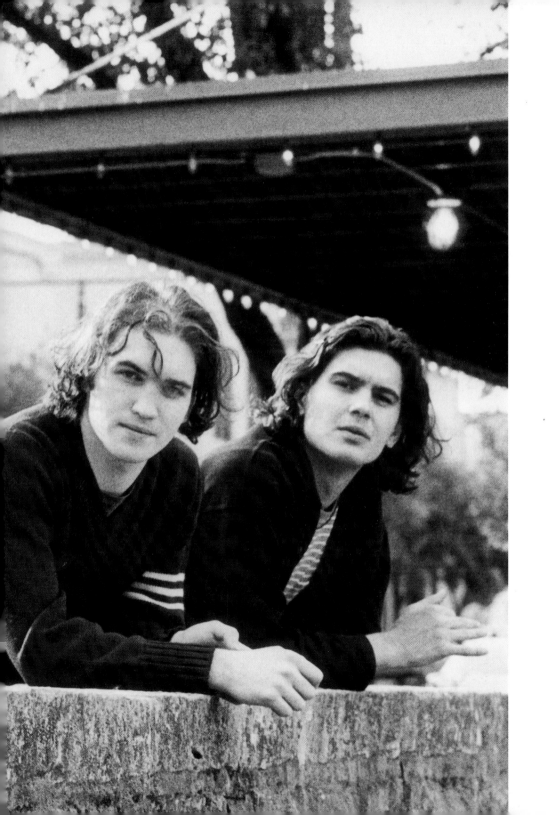

I wished for what happened in the making of *Grace* to happen for him again thirty more times. I'm telling you, as Mickey and Matty and Andy Wallace can attest to, what happened in basically a week was mind blowing. All of a sudden, what I thought was in there opened up. All of a sudden he opened the faucet. Out gushed the string arrangement, multilayered vocals and these guitar sounds, all of a sudden he whipped it out. All of a sudden this was like a different band and a guy who had gone from one level of output up to this whole other notch. Andy and I were looking at each other: "Is this happening? Andy, the tape's rolling, right?" An unbelievable transformation. It was one of the most incredible outbursts of creativity that I'd ever witnessed in my life. He goes over to the string arrangements and starts erasing things and writing things in for parts for eight strings. I'm going, I didn't know he knew this. He knew all about orchestrating and charting and arrangements and understood the harmonies enough on paper and pencil to hear all the harmonies in his head and change them. Carl Berger, who's the conductor of the Frankfurt Philharmonic Orchestra, is looking at this kid in ripped T-shirt and pants that are literally hanging off his butt writing the string

arrangements and then Carl Berger looks at him and goes, "Ja. Zis vill verk. 'S'good." And they played 'em all over again and Jeff rewrote the string parts. It's unbelievable.

I just thought that he had so much talent with so much hope for a long run. We're in a business where we eat the young immediately. This was a case where both I and the company thought and supported him in a way where, "Let this happen, let this go on." Very out of the ordinary of how people get signed. "What songs does he have, what's going to go on radio, what do we do with MTV?" These were not the initial questions asked. It was kind of like, "What direction do you think he might go in?" And the answer was, "We don't know." No one expected the album *Grace* to get made, because it didn't exist before it was made. I mean there wasn't a band six weeks before we would go and start to record.

—*Steve Berkowitz*

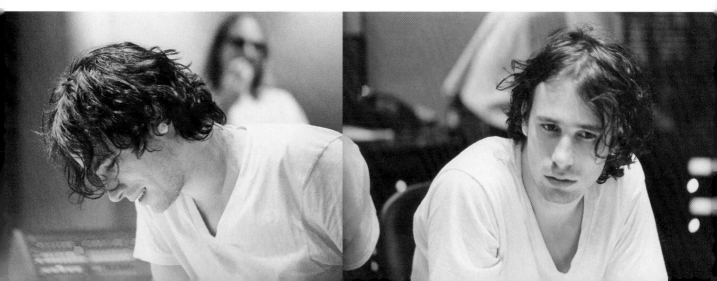

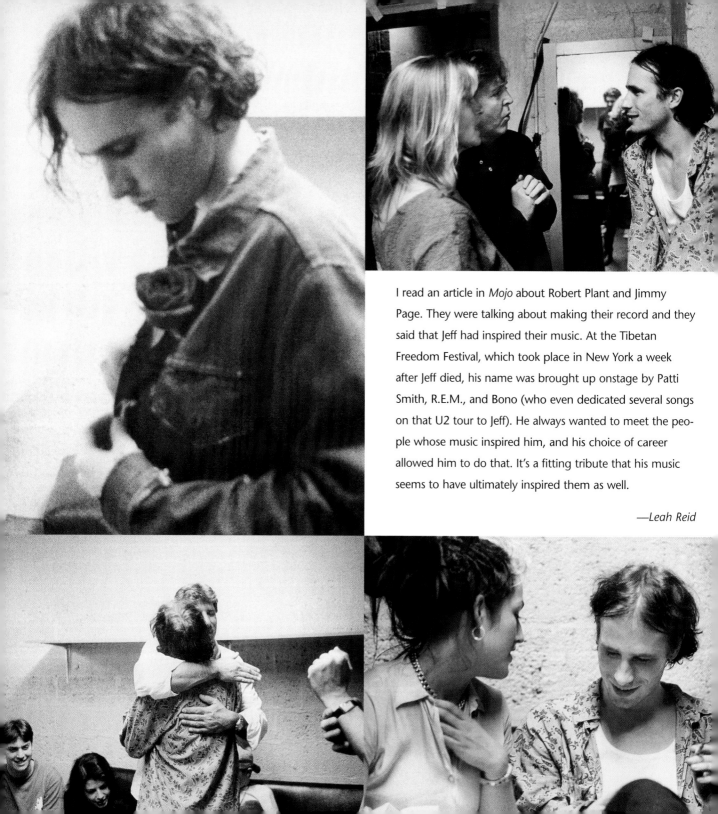

I read an article in *Mojo* about Robert Plant and Jimmy Page. They were talking about making their record and they said that Jeff had inspired their music. At the Tibetan Freedom Festival, which took place in New York a week after Jeff died, his name was brought up onstage by Patti Smith, R.E.M., and Bono (who even dedicated several songs on that U2 tour to Jeff). He always wanted to meet the people whose music inspired him, and his choice of career allowed him to do that. It's a fitting tribute that his music seems to have ultimately inspired them as well.

—Leah Reid

Jeff and I were traveling in London. It was the first show he had ever done in London and John McEnroe ended up carrying his amp down the stairs from upstairs at the Garage, which had a really long tall thin staircase. He lugged it into the cab for Jeff. Later, Chrissie Hynde wanted Jeff to go play with the Pretenders and Jeff was a BIG fan. So we're walking on the sidewalk and I was like a third wheel and Chrissie turned around and said, "Do you mind? I'd like to be alone with Jeff." He had a great time. He jammed with them playing old Pretenders hits. It was a really big deal to him.

—Dave Lory

He would hop on my tour if he wasn't on tour. He jumped in the back of our van once and ended up staying on for a week. I think he loved traveling because he traveled so much inside himself. It was just in his blood. He was living and moving inside music all the time. He'd wonder, "Why can't I be doing this every night?'

—Joan Wasser

Michael Tighe: It was sort of like a tryout. I didn't have a strap for my guitar and I was sitting down. At that point I had only played with friends and written a few songs in the last year of high school, but I hadn't really stood up and played much. We played for a while, and then it was all of a sudden over and it was very warm and I remember Jeff smiling.

Matt Johnson: And I remember it was a secret for a day or two as to whether or not you were going to be in the band. I remember I wanted to tell you so much. When we took a walk . . .

Michael: . . . we were trying to find a bank machine . . .

Matt: . . . and I was like no, don't do it . . . maybe you're the guitar player . . .

Michael: When I look at these pictures it reminds me of the speed and love that life took on when we were all together.

I never once heard him play the songs

that were on the record during

rehearsal. He goes, "Don't worry about

it, we'll be fine." I went out with Steve

Berkowitz to the first show, I was just sit-

ting there when they were going up

onstage going, "Oh my God, what's

going to come out of these amps?" And

it was great. The songs were there. But I

never once heard him play the songs off

the record during rehearsal.

—Dave Lory

It was interesting observing the transition Jeff made from his solo performances to the shows with the full band. One thing that set him apart from other solo acts was his uncanny ability to focus on and then respond to the mood and thoughts of the members of the audience. He'd overhear a snatch of conversation and put in his two cents on the subject or launch into a song relevant to the topic at hand. Or a song that was an ironic retort! What would have distracted other performers proved to be inspiration to him. This was something he'd talk about a lot, being aware of the vibe in the room and his overall emotional "groove" and who's in control. If he encountered a noisy, inattentive crowd, he'd deliberately back away from the mike and turn down his guitar so you could barely hear him and suddenly the room would go dead silent. If the audience was too reverent, he'd challenge them with a coarse joke. If they were excited and involved he'd egg them on with more and more passionate singing and playing. Jeff "playing the room" was an amazing phenomenon to witness.

When he assembled, his focus shifted from the audience to them. His attention moved from the vibe amongst audience members to what the other guys in the band were feeling and playing. He was incredibly attentive to tiny inflections in the rhythmic feel and melodic shapes they spin, constantly revising his own work in reaction to their playing. He encouraged them to adopt the same responsiveness and flexibility and when they were all "on" the results were transcendent. The results were an interactive, ever-changing tapestry. The fierce intimacy of the audience was lessened by this redirection of his focus, but the music produced was well worth the sacrifice.

—Howard Wuelfing

Part of what was so beautiful about Jeff was that he touched everybody; he was very affectionate. His relationship with friends, male or female, lovers, musicians, audience members, it was the same. People got the same thing. That's a beautiful thing and it moves people.

That's the reason why so many people were in love with him, why so many people thought he was in love with them. And I believe he was, wholeheartedly, but he didn't have enough of himself to give. His inclination was to engage everybody.

—Nicholas Hill

Michael Tighe: He liked to talk on the phone a lot, 'cause it was this very specific reality where he wasn't actually with the person but it was very intimate at the same time.

Matt Johnson: I remember once in Stockholm he got on the phone and he just started talking, I think I have a picture of him on the phone that day. He didn't realize that calling from Europe to America on the hotel phone without using a calling card costs an exorbitant amount of money. What happened is that he talked for so long that by the time he hung up the phone we tried to check out of the hotel and it was like . . . $1,500.

There was anger, sometimes, at the business. I don't think he ever came to terms. He was angry at the dynamics of the business, the expectation and pressure to sell a lot of records. No one was pressuring him to sell a lot of records but that was what the machinery was about. The star. There was part of him that enjoyed that, but there was another part of Jeff that was disgusted with it because it was commerce, that he was part of it.

—*George Stein*

I met him because he found out that I was from Pakistan. Penny told him that I was from the town Nusrat Fateh Ali Khan was born, so he sought me out, you know? I used to go all the time to Sin-é. Even when he was not singing we used to sit outside, there was a bench and we would just sit and talk and talk and talk. His sounds were connected with my birth, that's how I saw Jeff. All of the greatest Qawwali music was born in my town. They had this incredible soul, their music is very spiritual. They don't sing in order to become famous. These people just sang. They sang because it was part of their soul and this inside experience of their worth, and their ancestors, and their air and their flowers. It's a religious singing also, Qawwali, they could sing all night and not lose their voice. This music goes on all night, you know? What made them sing was not this whole commercial bullshit. They sang because they had to sing. That's what was so really attractive about Jeff for me, I just feel that our blood was together.

I think he felt like an outsider. The amazing thing is that he was born here, he was a young guy. Everything between us was different that way. He had hope in front of him. He's young, he's beautiful, he's a fabulous singer, he is making it. But I think he felt really like an outsider, with his work he was an outsider. Because his work was connected to another world which this world doesn't really understand, though he has lots of fans, you know? But the commercial world . . . I think since he was becoming famous, this incredible amount of pressure was already upon him. This was another reason why he did not want to tape the CD here and he went to Memphis to hide, you know, to hide. Everybody was after him because now he's becoming famous, and his music was very spiritual. He didn't want to belong to that [commercial] part of the world, but at the same time he wanted his work to be out. So this is where the conflict lies. He wanted to project out into the world, but he did not want to be a part of that world.

—*Bina Shariff*

I was friends with the Grifters. Jeff's band came, I think it was in February, and they played two gigs, this was when they were working with Tom Verlaine. They played at Barristers and afterwards he and I and some of the Grifters, and girlfriends . . . everybody wanted to go, because everybody wanted to be close to Jeff. We went to a bar called the P&H Café. I knew some other people there, and I spent the whole evening in other conversations around the room. At the end of the night Tripp and I were taking Jeff home to his room at the Claridge House and I had to go to the girls' room and Jeff had to go to the boys' room. We both came out of the rest rooms at the same time and we spontaneously karate-kicked the air, and he ran in the girls' room and I ran in the boys' room. And then we came out and kicked each other again, but not really. Then we got in the backseat of Tripp's car and like, that was just it, if you know what I mean. And so we were friends.

—*Andria Lisle*

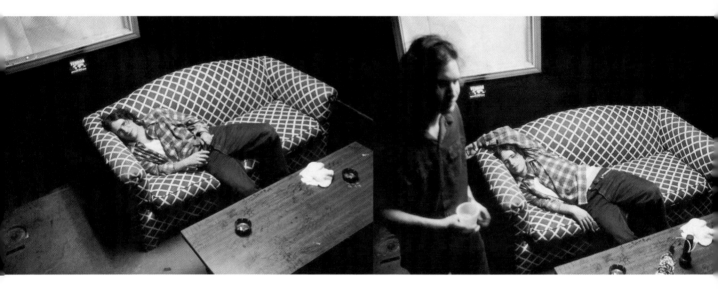

I know now that it's a serious thing, creating music. Jeff was the very first person to point out that Sufism and music and religion, and how being a musician is a very noble thing 'cause you're taking people away from their pain for a minute. We talked about concerts and how they were spiritual and religious gatherings. How with Nusrat Fateh Ali Khan people would throw roses and money at his feet, he was a deity in his homeland. Jeff was like, "When you listen to an Iggy Pop record doesn't it make you feel better? Of course! They want to see Iggy and they want to hear Iggy 'cause this is the man that makes 'em feel better . . . You're making people feel better, isn't that a noble thing?" For the first time in my life, I was like, "Hey, yeah!" I always thought that if I enjoy it, it must be selfish, and I'm not doing something good. I never thought about it like that . . .

—Inger Lorre

I just miss him schlumping in, any time, my receptionist buzzing me. "Jeff's here."

—*George Stein*

It was funny, you know, because when they all came in the room that night the club was very crowded. It was really funny because not a lot of people in Memphis knew who Jeff was but everybody KNEW, in capital letters, that this was a very big deal. So there were lots of people at the club and I'd never met Jeff before even though he'd been here in previous years. And I thought Mickey was Jeff when Mickey came in the room because Jeff was so little and lost looking. Mickey was this big strapping handsome lad checking out all the girls. Jeff came in with his little backpack on and a little ski cap, a little rat boy. So a couple days later he called and asked if I could take him to get his driver's license. I said to Jeff, come meet me and Luther Dickinson at Ardent, 'cause I didn't actually have a car at the time either, and Tripp has a car that we call the Town Drunk car because it's just really beat up. I was like if you can get to mid-town then I can probably get the Town Drunk car. He showed up in a cab right when Luther and I were finishing and we all went to lunch. At lunch Jeff was talking. Luther was scribbling in this notebook I have while Jeff talked and all of a sudden I think Jeff got really paranoid that Luther was taking notes on him. Jeff had been telling us the story about camping with his mother and his grandmother and how the grandmother would call him "stinky feet." So he reaches across the table and wrenches the book out of Luther's hands and there's a drawing of a pair of feet, and it says "stinky feet."

We were eating at this little soul food restaurant and Jeff ordered two main dishes. They kept asking him if he realized that was what he'd ordered, and he said "Yeah." And when the food came everyone came out of the kitchen to watch this little boy eat this giant meal.

I think some nights he would go eat dinner at three or four people's houses and be a different stray kitten at each house.

Jeff's house had no furniture. Every time I went over there his bed was in a different room. Gene [Bowen] had gone and rented furniture and he had to buy sheets for the bed. There was nothing. Mickey [Grondahl] I think was gonna stay with me because it was the beginning of summer and Jeff had no air-conditioning. And he had had some discussions I think about the wildness, about camping out at Jeff's.

We took Jeff to Green's Lounge, which is this really wonderful club where we would go dance on Saturday nights, a black club. He would wear layer upon layer of clothes and by the end of the night he'd be in a wife beater, like an old man's under-shirt, and his trousers jumping up and down while the band did James Brown.

coming and I walked my dog over there and he really wanted to go. Foti was there, and Gene. He was like "I wanna go, what time would we be back?" and I said, "Midnight." He was like, "Well, the boys are coming and I want to go play the drums." He was really excited. So the verdict was that Jeff would stay home and that I would go to the casinos, then when I got back I would come tell him how much I won and pick up Mickey to come over here to go to sleep. I walked my dog over there at about twelve-thirty and there were voices inside and they said, "Who's there?" and I said, "It's Andria." And they said, "Who's with you?" And I said, "My dog." And they said, "Go away." And I was perturbed and I was like, ugh . . . musicians. I just thought they were having a discussion. I didn't think another thing about it and I went home and went to sleep and I went to work the next day. My boss asked me if I was with Jeff the night before and I said yeah and he said, "No you weren't." And I said, "Yeah," and he asked again and I said, "Yeah," and at that point the phone rang and it was a fellow from the newspaper wanting a comment about his death. It was just awful. It was awful because all these people were saying all these awful things, and he was so happy. The whole time I was friends with him I really wanted to be careful about not counting on him too much or not being too good of friends with him because I was like, he's gonna leave. Because I'm always friends with people who are in transit. I want to say this in the right way because it was completely platonic, but not falling in love with him too much as a friend. Because he was so wonderful and he made everyone that was with him feel so on top of the world. Just the way he would look at you whether you were a boy or a girl or a dog or a fireman. He made you so happy and we had so much fun. I would give anything not to know him and have him be alive. It was so bittersweet knowing that he was going to buy that house and he was going to stay here, because then I wouldn't have lost my friend.

—Andria Lisle

...en he just kind of came home with us and he never went ...d got his driver's license that day, and he just stayed over ...ere for three days. My roommate and I were really amused. I ...ave a dog and she has a stuffed shark and he would wear it ...his armpit and walk around the house singing Metallica ...pera style squeezing the dog toy as a percussion instrument. ...e dog, of course would follow him from room to room. At ...e point we were on the balcony and he asked where ...mbert Street was because he was about to get his house ...d I said, "It's right on the other side of those trees." And he ...id, "Oh, we're going to be neighbors." And then I said, ...eff, you can't come over here anymore," [laugh] and he just ...d the saddest look on his face. I liked to tease him a lot just ...cause he was so sincere and he was really sweet. You know ...hat I mean.

...was the night before and I was going to a casino with some ...ends. He and I talked a lot about going down there for free ...inks. We talked about it but that was the night the band was

RAUSCH

I loved seeing it happen to people. I loved people not knowing who he was and then at the end of the show being transfixed and transformed. I loved that. I watched the rabidity of the fans develop. He had the ability to make every person feel, even if it was for one second, that they were the most important person in the universe. It was his way of being able to reach out and touch somebody for one second and thank them, by a touch or a glance, for being a fan and appreciating his music. It was how he gave something back to them. Sometimes people would take those moments the wrong way, or would try and take more than he could possibly give. Some people became obsessive. There were actually a couple of times when I had to protect him from people. He would say, "Hold my hand," or he would put his arm around me to put some sort of barrier between him and people. At a certain point, he sort of closed himself off, because people wanted pieces of him that he wouldn't give. Shouldn't give.

—Leah Reid

I think my goals with Jeff were: number one, for him to have his own personal life where people left him alone. I think the first thing was to allow him space to be his own person because I think the thing that was most frustrating for him was to come back to New York. He was checking his messages for an hour and a half. It was like seventy-something messages. Number two was to protect him where he owned himself. George, Victor, and I did a great job. He owned all of his companies, he signed all of his checks, he got his accounting monthly. I'd sit him down with it and of course that was like going to the dentist. But he always knew what was going on and he ran Jeff Buckley Enterprises. Nobody else did. Number three was, we were just a catalyst. Meaning he did whatever he wanted and our job was to provide him with what he wanted in order to accomplish those goals, as crazy as they may seem. That's what we did for him.

When we sat down with Jeff, we said this is how the business works. We never dictated to Jeff what to do. If you want to do it the way that he wanted to do it, which was, "I want the music for the people" and no edits [radio], then you need to play live. You need to hit markets three times if you're not going to have radio in order to have an impact. We gave him three or four choices and he picked touring, and then we worked that system. We did the marketing plan around that. The whole thing with Jeff was, record one was to get him off tour support so he'd be free, meaning if he got in a fight with the record company and didn't want to release a record he could tour for the rest of his life. He wouldn't need to do anything, he was totally self-sufficient. We accomplished that on the first record. That was our goal. The second record was to get him to recoupment, and the third record was to have him explode and be an international superstar. That's a bad word, but nonetheless, he would have been huge. We always knew he'd write a hit one day. We figured between the second and third record he'd do that.

—Dave Lory

The way you could entice Jeff was with food. He was always hungry. Sometimes we'd get in the car and go out to City Island and go sit by the water and talk. I learned that I shouldn't put on the radio if Jeff was in the car with me because he would just focus so much on the radio and play with the dial like he'd never seen a radio before. He couldn't resist it, you'd lose him . . . It was a very funny thing.

—George Stein

One night, we were out at the Hard Rock Café, eating hamburgers. He casually looked around the restaurant, looking left and right. He grabbed a bottle of ketchup, and looked around again. He put the bottle up to his mouth, pierced the metal cap of the bottle with his fang tooth, showed it to me, and put the bottle back on the table. He actually had the ability to pierce metal with his teeth.

—Leah Reid

Jeff had tried to order some french fries at the
bar and the bar was like, no more food, we're
going home. They didn't care who he was
either. So he was walking around the room eating fries off of abandoned plates. And he had
the saddest look on his face. He was playing the
Grifters on the jukebox and his song had finally
come on and it was two in the morning and the
bar was going home and they unplugged the
jukebox in the middle of his song. Jeff leapt up
on the pool table with his mouth full of french
fries and he started shouting, "Grifters! Grifters!"
spitting food all over the place. And this friend
of mine Jason was with us, his eyes were as wide
as saucers. What is this little creature?

—*Andria Lisle*

He played a version of "Indifference" for me. Man I tell you, I'll never forget the way he did it ... I was just fuckin' speechless ... one of the most memorable moments of my life.

—Eddie Vedder of Pearl Jam, on *Monkeywrench Radio*

Matt Johnson: It was maybe six months after *Grace* had been tracked that we recorded "So Real," it was sort of a snap decision and it replaced this song that Jeff really despised. Mike wrote the music . .

Michael Tighe: . . . and Jeff wrote the melody and the words. He only had the choruses for a long time, there was nothing of the verse and we had tracked the songs. It was really really late at night, we were at the studio and I went out with Chris Dowd down to the corner or something, and then Jeff went for a walk. When we got back, he had already done one pass of the whole song, with the verses. I guess he'd had it floating around in his head and it was realized when he went for that quick walk. He did all of the verses in one take.

Matt: We had this other phase and we were rehearsing and it was for eons. We were at Montana [studios] for years [laugh]. We were going there and improvising between tours. We would go in there for part of the day and drink coffee and play. We did "The Morning After" and we did "Tongue" . . . Remember? That's a really beautiful piece. It was on some European release. That actually exhibits a lot of what the band dynamic was, the way we worked together, a very subtle consistent structured kind of way. The way Jeff would be very atmospheric. Michael's parts were very pulsating, almost like a skeleton.

Michael: Mick would be very fluid, interacting with Jeff's voice.

Matt: I remember one time when we were playing at the Fez, and I remember feeling a kind of shock of amazement and joy, feeling the generation of energy. It was amazing. It was very interpretive, based on the room and based on the way each person felt. Based on the audience. And some of the ways we'd interpret the songs would actually end up how we would play the arrangements. The arrangements would change based on what would happen when we were playing. It was definitely not like we were just re-creating the record by any means. I always thought of it like playing ball. The ball game like a metaphor. The focal point at any given moment was just sort of passed around from person to person. We learned to have balance with each other. To trust each other. Kind of like . . . resonate with each other.

I remember the very first time playing with Jeff. I was like, "Damn, that little Fender amp's loud!" It blew out my left ear. All of it was right there in the very beginning. It was beautiful. Gorgeous, the playing . . . He just liked to get to that volume with the cymbals, at the high end of the amps, and he created this silvery sound like a sonic superstructure. It was like this halo around the music with all the overtones, incredibly beautiful and very metallic, very hard to deal with physically. Very beautiful. He'd go for that solo too, with his twelve-string. Twelve strings through an amp. Just, like, unbelievable . . .

His voice had all the melody of the ghazal—the ghazal is a sonnet, but it's very tragic and it's deep. Very, very deep. It runs from the depth of your soul, and that's what he had. It is a very classical format of old, old Indian Muslim music. If you watch people who understand the ghazal they just sit there and something happens to them, to be moved to another experience. Nothing else matters then. Those people feel so connected and content with the gift of birth. They feel so in gratitude to the person who's singing the ghazal, because that person is the god. That person is the one who is the spirituality of your soul. You just thank God for the existence, that you were born so you could hear this, and you feel that God is sending you a gift. So he was the gift for me in this country, he was my gift.

—*Bina Shariff*

I think Jeff was someone who was working his way backward in his life, as everybody does, to figure out who he was and how he actually wanted to be. He was working very hard at that. I think it was the primary thing that was going on in his life. He was straightening out his own psychology. Being a rock star was not the number-one thing that was going on in the guy's life. Straightening out his own philosophy and own mind was his number-one priority.

—*Penny Arcade*

Jeff dug touring. He was comfortable on the road. Maybe he did allow the touring to go on longer than was best for him. He told me that he'd moved around a lot as a kid so the mobile lifestyle was natural for him. On the other hand, settling down in New York, having his own home and neighborhood were good, centering things for him. But the road offered up a world of other opportunities for experience and he always loved encountering the fresh and novel. Exploring. Being surprised. Meeting new people and finding out about their lives and experiences. I don't know that all that was "good" for him but I do believe that he was having the time of his life.

—Howard Wuelfing

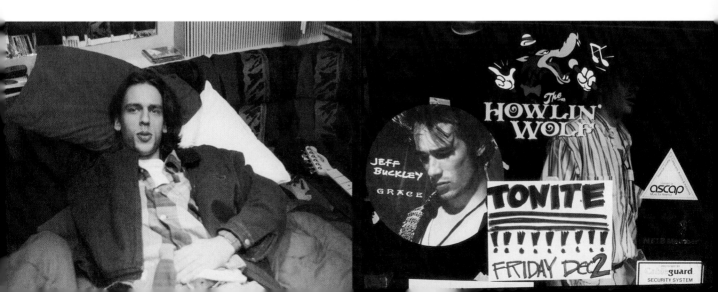

The album that I've been listening to for the last eighteen months is *Grace* by Jeff Buckley. He is a great, great singer. He has such an emotional range, doing songs by Benjamin Britten and Leonard Cohen as well as his own—such technique and command.

When the Page/Plant tour hit Australia, we saw them and we were knocked out. It was very moving. Someone heckled him from the audience—"Stop playing that heavy stuff!"—but he made the perfect reply: "Music should be like making love—sometimes you want it soft and tender, other times you want it hard and aggressive." I felt he paid us a great compliment with his music in that style.

—Jimmy Page,
Mojo, January 1997

Most of us are comfortable socializing on an ongoing basis with, say, twenty people. Jeff's "circle of friends" was more like twenty hundred. He had warm relations with people from the East Coast to the West, to Europe to Australia thanks to the long period when he toured ceaselessly and his extraordinary ability to connect with people, instantly and deeply. I don't know if the constant socializing sustained him emotionally. I think that came through taking his thoughts and feelings and making them into songs. It appeared to me that his songs were a diagnostic and therapeutic exercise for him. They gave him the chance to examine and critique his inner experiences.

—Howard Wuelfing

He had a real talent and a genuine need when he met someone to really give them his full attention. And I think it was genuine, that when you were with Jeff, you had his full attention and vividly felt that he was utterly enthralled by you. He made you feel unique. Because it was kind of unusual to be treated that way by someone, people would misinterpret that intensity and get confused when five minutes later he was equally focused on someone else. He treated everyone that way: bag ladies, rock stars, industry bigwigs—no matter how brief or long the time he spent with them. It felt really good and it seemed that a lot of people didn't have an easy time sharing him.

—*Howard Wuelfing*

He was afraid that the audiences were the same assholes that were jerks to him in high school. He had a lot of trouble in high school as the little skinny musician with all those jocks and he would get the shit kicked out of him. His nightmare was that they were in front of him as his fans. That tortured him.

—*George Stein*

He was a pure drop in an ocean of noise. Jeff Buckley's voice reminds me of the old Salvation Army hymn

"Amazing Grace, how sweet the sound." Grace as a signature. Grace personified in one man's vibrato—a

delicate tremulous voice which rightfully betrays its Middle Eastern tutelage.

Jeff was trained in Sufi singing. His ululating voice reminds me how few singers there are in rock 'n' roll.

—*Bono,* Propaganda, *December 1999*

The most interesting thing for me was seeing him play in small places, Cornelia Street Café, Skep, and Sin-é, the teeny places with just a couple of people in the audience. What he was doing, consciously, was abandoning any songs that he had written and discovering the core of the music that he loved, what made the great songs great. He would dig into them and perform them over and over in different ways every single time. He was on a quest. It was like a study course for him. He was really investigating something with great discipline. He didn't need an audience. He might, say, go to Sin-é at the end of the night and just start doing a set. You never really knew when he would be playing, but he was there a lot, washing dishes, drinking his coffee, doing a gig.

—Nicholas Hill

I took him to a gig in Oxford, Mississippi, one night, and all these Ol' Miss sorority girls were inviting them over to their house

for a party. He opened up for a swing band, the bill didn't go together at all. The first song the band played was "Losers Waltz"

and Jeff turned to me and he said, "Shall we dance, madam?" and I said, "Of course." And he purposefully fell off his bar stool,

like the Tin Man in *The Wizard of Oz*, and hit the ground and bounced back up. By the time we were dancing around the room

none of the girls were there anymore. They were just horrified . . .

Even working at a record store, I was so naive about him. I wanted to protect him. In my journal entries from then, I could count

on my fingers and toes the number of times we hung out. It was a brief period of time. Like three months. You know, I went to

New York and I really wanted to go just for the process of grieving. I'm in New York at Jeff's memorial and you know, Elvis

Costello is sitting in front of me and Marianne Faithfull is performing. And I'm like, no, this was this kid Jeff that lives down the

street. I had no idea. This was the kid who couldn't afford a car and rode a bicycle.

He could definitely be himself, or be whichever self he wanted to be. Memphis is easy and comfortable and I don't think people were too concerned. It's a very easy town to live in without too much money. I know he was talking to Gene about getting his affairs in order to the point where he could handle them himself. But it's a great town, a lot cheaper than New York, so I think he thought he could be here and not really bother anybody and sit at home and record, he didn't have a lot of needs while he was here. Joan would come and they would lie in the yard in the weeds, he never mowed his yard so when they'd lie in the yard you couldn't even tell anyone was home. They would just hide like that for days.

He was schizophrenic in a good way. I mean, he was always an actor. The last week he was here I was going to get lunch and he was coming out of this Mexican restaurant and he saw me walking down the street and so he started prancing down the street like a fairy. And I said, "Jeff, someone's going to pull over in a pickup truck and kill you, just like the end of *Easy Rider* they're gonna shoot you off your bike." He thought that was hilarious. I felt really awful because I warned him about everything except for the river.

—*Andria Lisle*

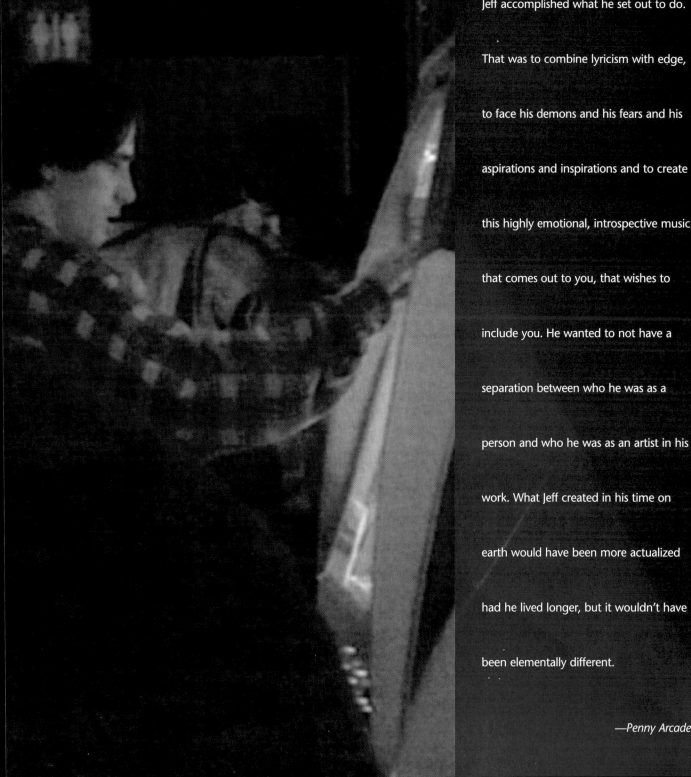

Jeff accomplished what he set out to do.

That was to combine lyricism with edge,

to face his demons and his fears and his

aspirations and inspirations and to create

this highly emotional, introspective music

that comes out to you, that wishes to

include you. He wanted to not have a

separation between who he was as a

person and who he was as an artist in his

work. What Jeff created in his time on

earth would have been more actualized

had he lived longer, but it wouldn't have

been elementally different.

—*Penny Arcade*

Jeff was always jumping off a cliff and halfway down I'd

look at him and say, "Do you have a parachute?" and

he'd go, "Yeah, I think so." My opinion of that para-

chute would be that he would pull out a dirty Kleenex,

and knowing Jeff, it'd open up. That's how he made his

decisions, that's how he ran with his music, and I

unconditionally backed him on that. And that's what

was fun about working with Jeff. I think that was what

was the beauty about him, but he was like a freight

train out of control, he just kept getting better and

better and better.

—*Dave Lory*

I was sweating like a fucking June bride when I first heard him. Music has never done that to me before.

—*Elizabeth Fraser, Cocteau Twins*

I see him in that coat with his hands in his pockets
and just sort of looking a bit impish,
but very deep at the same time.

They were starting one of the European tours in January of '95. We began in Dublin and the American company had kept him behind for a Hall of Fame dinner or something. The band and Gene [Bowen] had flown on to Dublin and the only way to get Jeff there on time was if Columbia paid for him to fly on the Concorde to London late the previous night. I was living in London at the time not that far from the airport. I was going out to Dublin for the tour so I met him off the plane, and bless him, he just . . . huh . . . I just stood there in this sort of sterile terminal at Heathrow and these people got off the Concorde in their skycaps and their Gucci luggage or Louis Vuitton bags or whatever and I was thinking . . . I bet he missed the plane. It wouldn't have really surprised me. Then off he came with his little black guitar case and a black furry coat and hat and a little daisy in his lapel looking like Paddington Bear. I just wanted to hug him. I actually stayed at the hotel at the airport with him under strict instructions not to let him go wandering off into town and getting trashed or whatever. You know, otherwise he would sleep over and not make the plane. It was 'round midnight by the time we had gotten to the hotel. And the minute we got there he was like, "Okay Sammy, can I go out now please?" And I just sat there and was like, "Don't do this to me, please . . . don't put me in this position." And this is why I'd probably been elected to do it. I was like, "Gene and Dave will kill me." He said, "I can't sleep, I just want to go and see a friend." I'm like, "Okay, on two conditions. One, you don't tell Dave and Gene. And two, you take my mobile phone and you call me every so often if you're going to be late. And call me when you want a car to come and pick you up and bring you back 'cause I want to know that you're here so that we're going to make that flight the next morning." And he did. I felt like I was his mother trying to get on with a teenager that you're trying to keep on the right track. I remember the next morning we got up and trundled back to the airport and of course he'd lost his ticket, I had to buy him a new ticket. I think he actually lost a guitar as well, but we found it later on. And then we flew to Dublin.

—Sam Way

Jeff didn't seem to spend enough time involved in the things that appeared to sustain him the most, like making new music . . . making it for pure and possibly esoteric reasons. He didn't spend enough time immersing himself in it and indulging his creative impulses. He became too concerned about how other people would perceive this or that piece of music instead of just belting it out, laying it down on a cassette deck at home and then figuring out what to do with it: bring this song to the label, give that one away to a friend's group, save another for a foreign B-side. After the first album was released, he seemed to spend all his time laboring over the same batch of ideas, reworking them *ad nauseam*. Not all creative impulses are great and worth being brought to fruition. But he seemed determined to perfect and polish it all and figure out how to make it work and work fabulously, not just passably. He set himself a difficult, inherently frustrating task here.

It seemed he was also conflicted about his relationship with the rest of the band. There was no doubt that he loved them and the ensemble sound that they created as a unit was a rare and wonderful thing that few rock groups even conceive of let alone achieve. So on one hand, he wanted to be one member of a group and for everyone to contribute. Which as players they unquestionably did. When he tried having everyone write as a group, hunkering down in a beach one winter however, it just didn't work. In the end, *he* had a vision and it was that vision that the music had to embody. I don't know. Maybe he figured that the other band members were so immersed and committed to his music that they naturally would contribute things in perfect harmony with it rather than have their own unique ideas. And their ideas per se were not part of his vision. I believe that the experience was very disappointing to him and it seemed to take him a long time after abandoning the group writing before he settled down to composing on his own again, but when he did he created more beautiful, strange, utterly unique music that finally showed up on *Sketches* (for *My Sweetheart the Drunk*).

—Howard Wuelfing

I felt very paternal and very protective because I knew how absolutely vulnerable he was. I felt I was there to assure him that no one in the business was going to take advantage of him and that he was going to be all right. I constantly had to tell him that he wasn't going to make the same mistakes that his father made. That haunted him. As it got busier and more people were pulling on him we couldn't see each other as much because he was traveling, but it was just a relationship built on trust. I was there from the beginning to the end, which was a long time. I guess it was '91 to '97. From playing for tips at Sin-é to traveling around the world to Australia to Japan to England, where he was a demigod. It was quite a ride. That's why I'm so proud of that tour poster that he signed over there. He wrote on the poster, "George, there from the beginning, here to the end. Thank you for all you do, thank you for everything in between. What is Yiddish for you rock? This is you. Jeff." This is sweet, but, it wasn't supposed to turn out this way, so it's bittersweet.

—*George Stein*

Just after Jeff died, I had an amazing dream . . .

I dreamt I was in his apartment. It was dark and as my eyes adjusted I began to see all the ordinary things of life, of Jeff's life, in the room . . . shirts hung over the back of a chair, books everywhere, some opened, some written on, papers on the bed, pictures on the walls . . . I walked through this room and into another smaller room. On a little dresser against the wall, there was an old-style child's music box, the kind with a ballerina that turns around in front of a little mirror. I opened the box, and there was no ballerina, but instead in the mirror was the word LOVE written in seventies bubble letters. After a moment I realized the word was backwards, as if I were LOVE being reflected in the mirror. Suddenly, I felt so happy. And that's how it was with Jeff. Somehow he was that mirror, always reflecting back the love inside you.

—*Brenda Kahn*

All along he was willing to say fuck you to the business. When you look at that video of "Last Goodbye," at the very end he looks at the video camera really pissed off. That is not an act. He was so pissed off that he had to do that video.

—*George Stein*

Jeff moved really fast, like he was experiencing life at a very high speed and just really playful, like a kid, but with some very strong secret and internal language that he had with himself. There was one area that was really intangible. You could look in his eyes sometimes and know he was reverberating inside himself, that he had these emotions and ideas that he probably would never tell anybody.

—*Michael Tighe*

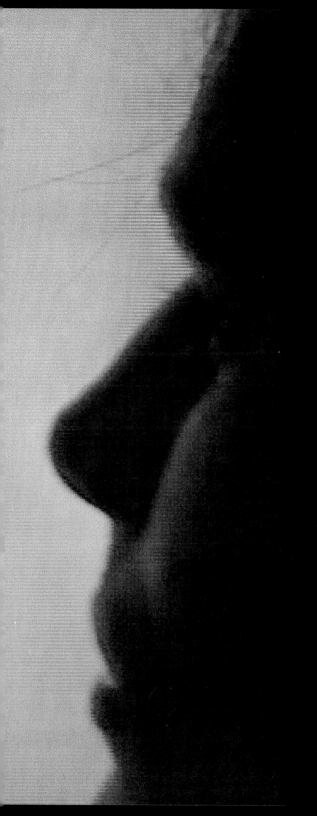

He was enjoying being somewhat unnoticed in Memphis. It wasn't like being in New York City. He could be a bit more anonymous. Most of the people didn't know who he was, nor did they care, which was nice for him. I got there and he lived in this empty wooden house . . . I don't think anybody went down. Dave Lory went once. The band never went, I went three times. It was my job to, and because I wanted to. We spent two days in that house by ourselves and he didn't have tape recorders and stuff, but he did have a four-track, one amplifier, one microphone, a couple of guitars, and some headphones. When I got there the amplifier was broken. We spent sixteen hours over two days listening to what he had put down on tape with me and my right ear on one headphone, his guitar between us, the left ear of the headphones on his ear listening to the songs. Sometimes he would sing along. He did a lot of the songs that people have now heard from the *Sketches* album, as he was attending them at that time. Me holding one headphone to me and one up to him . . . Neither one of us smelled very good, by the way, after two days of doing this at his house. I didn't stay at his house. As soon as I saw the fleas jumping around I wasn't going to stay there. I just came back and brought food and barbecue stuff for us to eat. We called up the Grifters, one of the guys in the Grifters and his wife who were really very nice, we went there for dinner one night and Jeff springs on her, "We're going to come over and record all night." She says, "No. You're not." He was convinced that he was ready. It was the first time in three years, he was ready to do this. And he really was, I think, on the verge of doing something spectacular. Over the next week and a half he finished a tape and then sent one to me, sent one to Joan, and sent one to the three guys in the band. Each tape different. Each different. He mixed each person's tape separately. So I got nine songs and discovered later from Parker that Parker got eight or nine different songs, and the songs that were the same, on mine he'd intro the songs, he would say the name of it, "Uh, 'Thousand Fold,' by Jeff Buckley." And then on Parker's song it might not be there and on the outro of the song he may have overdubbed laughter, on Parker's tape, or on Michael's tape.

—*Steve Berkowitz*

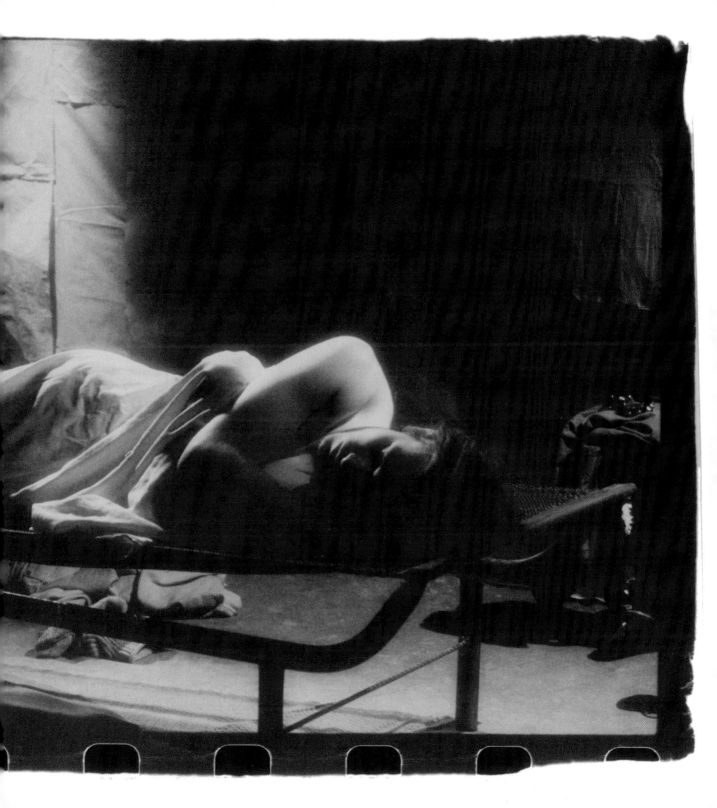

We went over to my parents' house for dinner one night, it was the night he played in Mississippi for the sorority girls. I had told my parents about him and they were used to me bringing home musicians or whatever. My mother . . . she loves every-one, and she loves everyone unconditionally. I wanted to take him out there so much because I wanted him to have that, because my mother's always been so gracious with friends of mine that were a little needy. I mean, she'd mend clothes and do laundry and feed them. Listen to stories. And what was so funny to me was that he was so taken by my dad, cause my dad was

like, "He sure was a funny little feller." When Jeff was there he talked about where Jeff Moorhead came from, where Scott came from, he talked about Mary, he talked about Peggy. And he laid out all these relationships and then a week later he died. It was really strange because I knew her name was Mary Guibert and why her name was Mary Guibert, you know what I'm saying? He spelled all of this stuff out for me, so that when they came . . .

there wasn't any confusion. I don't really know how to say what I'm trying to say. It's just really weird that he had the insight, for whatever reason, to lay all this out. It's just kind of funny.

—Andria Lisle

I hope that people who liked him resist the temptation to turn his life and death into some dumb romantic fantasy—he was so much better than that. Not everyone can get up and sing something they take a liking to and make it their own, sing true to their heart and be curious about all different strains of music. "Corpus Christi Carol" was a completely conceived interpretation. I'd never heard the piece before and when I heard the original I realized what Jeff had done was even more amazing. He'd taken it into his own world. That's something my favorite classical musicians can do, be themselves but use all that expertise to make the music more beautiful. Jeff did that naturally. Only a handful of people are capable of that.

—Elvis Costello, Mojo, *August 1997*

I think most of the time he felt like he was with his audience, not that they were necessarily there for him. Jeff was a very nice guy, though he often came off to some people as other than that. He was highly insecure about personal relationships, and he tried to give of himself all the time. Any discussion with Jeff was just you and him, which I think after his passing was so difficult for so many people to come to grips with because thousands of people thought they had an incredibly personal and intimate relationship with him. And I guess they did.

—Steve Berkowitz

I think he is touching people who are really true artists and who had gone through shit, and that actually he eventually said, "Fuck you all, I want to do my work." Because that's what counts, the work. People are very lonely and they're very sad and they have lots of tragedies in their lives they've never confronted. He made people confront certain things in themselves, but through the music.

To just go inside yourself. To see more of your own beauty from inside. I think that's why he had those devoted fans. Because they saw their own imagination and beauty and their own qualities in him. Jeff was real. The more he sang the more connection he had. He was too much of a bird, he was too beautiful.

—*Bina Shariff*

He definitely had a way to raise your spiritual consciousness. He made you look forward to things. He'd lift my spirits. A lot of the conversations would border on semi-spiritual . . . the goodness in you. But also there's a reality to it too . . .

He wanted to do things more on his own terms, going to the studio was his idea, doing the solo tour was his idea, making his ideas not so conventional and turn them into reality.

—*Jack Bookbinder*

He was naive and hungry for knowledge and experience. He was a little boy with huge, six-foot eyes, all black, no pupils, taking it all in. I don't think that people always understood him. I think that there were people who just went along with him, and people who were scared by him.

—*Leah Reid*

I truly believed that he was going to change the face of music. That's how much faith I had in his talent. I think that ultimately he has. When he came on the scene, there wasn't anyone that you could compare him to. He was "genre-less"—his music didn't quite fit anywhere. Now his music is used as a yardstick by which people compare other music. And now, I don't know how many times I hear that so-and-so has "the vocal stylings of Jeff Buckley," or that so-and-so is going to be "the next Jeff Buckley." The fact that his name is used in this way shows that he did really change music . . . and I think he will continue to do so.

—Leah Reid

Jeff was all about love. Everything came down to basically, love is the most powerful thing in the universe. Not turn the other cheek, but definitely love. Jeff was nobody's martyr, and I don't think he would like people turning him into the tragic young beautiful thing. I mean they're starting to martyr him now. He would hate that. You know he would hate it. He was very humble.

—Inger Lorre

He was intensely spontaneous, full of life, full of passion, everything was "the most." Everything either was the suckiest or it was the best. It was the most delicious, the most intoxicating, the most incredible or it sucked the worst anything could suck. When all the talk was going on about what music to let fans have after he died and people were saying, "Oh, he wanted to burn those tapes." Well, I'm sure he said that, and I'm sure he believed it the second he said that. Then, two seconds after, I'd guess that he didn't quite mean exactly the same thing. I do believe that he thought he could do better and he wanted the chance to do better. A strange fact is that those tapes that he allegedly wanted to burn, he did overdubs on . . . A lot of *My Sweetheart the Drunk* is him trying on different influences, which was his work method. But the references are so brief and flash by so quick and are strung together in a totally revolutionary way that no one who had ever referenced that same material achieved. And he put it together in a way that made it entirely 1,000 percent Jeff Buckley. Nothing else sounded like that.

—Howard Wuelfing